expressive
modern

expressive modern

THE INTERIORS OF AMY LAU

Written with Linda O'Keeffe

The Monacelli Press

Library of Congress Control Number: 2011927654
ISBN 9781580933087

Printed and bound in Singapore

10 9 8 7 6 5 4 3 2 1
First edition

www.monacellipress.com

Designed by Michelle Leong

To all my mentors and teachers,
and especially my amazing staff,
my dear family and friends, and
of course to my magic dragon, Mr. Goof,
and my rock Chris Klapper.

contents

introduction

As a child growing up in Northern Arizona, I had a heightened relationship, bordering on a dialogue, with my immediate surroundings. I was impulsively drawn to this color or that material. Certain spaces affected my mood and sense of well-being. Historic homes captivated me to the point where I could practically see the former occupants going about their daily business.

I loved building forts with the neighborhood boys and constructing model buildings, and also happily spent hours in museums enthralled by the minutiae of a painting. I would marvel at the intricacy of a bird's wing; I'd project a narrative onto a portrait. But at the end of the day, I figured I'd become a marine biologist or an archeologist, anything that kept me outdoors and in nature.

I see nature as a friend and teacher, a mentor who shaped my imagination early on and continues to inform my interior design work now. I grew up with a horse, White Eagle, and we considered the desert, in all its brutal beauty, to be our open-ended playground. I cherish those days riding bareback through the arroyos past saguaro cacti, Gila monsters, and roadrunners. It was pure, unadulterated adventure.

When you regularly commune with nature, intuition sharpens and a type of holistic vision develops. To this day, when I'm back in the desert, I can be bowled over by the myriad colors of earth while I'm conscious of cloud formations racing across the sky. As I appreciate the woven complexity of passing tumbleweed I'm also aware of the red clay canyons that appear sharp and close while they're actually three miles in the distance. That split-focus agility—to consider a detail and its larger context at one and the same time—is fundamental to a designer's work and is critical for working with architects on a daily basis. Our professions are truly two sides of the same coin.

Travel equally shapes and molds my vision. My family was privileged to own a beach house in San Diego as well as a condo in Santa Fe while we regularly vacationed in Telluride. I attended school in the Midwest, had dear friends in the South, and my parents' insistence that we explore as much of this country as possible before setting foot in Europe prompted my affection and broad respect for American regionalism. I was an exchange student in France, studied languages in Seville, art history and architecture in Greece and Italy, and I take off every summer to spend time in India, Turkey, or Beirut—the more exotic the place, the better. Art, literature, fashion, food, architecture, and colors from other cultures energize and replenish my senses while they sensitize my eye, providing a full-bodied experience.

There is something to be said for staying close to home, however. The closeness of my family and its homegrown creativity has also affected me. My grandmother and I used to walk along the beach with our heads craned downward, intent on finding the perfect shell, stone, or other sea-swept art supply we needed for the collages and miniature tableaus we'd make as soon as we returned home. I often feel like I channel her when I'm assembling collections for my clients. She was a lifelong painter, and she taught me how to look intensively at waves and capture their life force on paper.

My family is related to Oscar Berninghaus, a founder of the Taos Society of Artists, and my father collects paintings of that period as well as material culture, so art, in many forms, was a staple in our home. In Santa Fe, my dad was my gallery and museum buddy and we ventured off together to attend Pueblo dances, quietly watching, in awe of the ancient ceremonies. My mother still has a devotion to beauty and a hawk's eye for details. She organized and orchestrated our homes with unbelievable passion and precision. I was her right hand, dressing the table according to her directives, so she could serve an artfully arranged dinner at six o'clock on the dot. To paraphrase Stendhal, beauty is the promise of happiness.

I'm the only member of my family, over four generations, who no longer lives in Arizona. But even as a transplant to Manhattan, I'm rooted to the Southwest. I still think of its dusty olives, siennas, and rusted browns as "my colors." I've heard painters refer to New Mexico as the only place in America where true color exists and that's hard to dispute. Its sunsets are practically psychedelic as they scroll from purple to red to orange to gold to cerulean blue. Desert light, whether it's from the sun, moon, or stars, is optimistic and radiant. It has a discernible physicality, like a living, crystallized spirit that inhabits space and sharpens forms. I strive to reproduce that intensity of color and light in my work.

Soon after I earned my undergraduate art history degree, I embarked on a series of buying excursions in the heart of Mexico with Dino Alfaro, who runs Antigua de Mexico, his family's international decorative arts business. We negotiated directly with artisans in remote villages, appreciating the milky-white glazed Talavera pottery from Puebla, jewel-toned glass from Tonala, and copal woodcarvings from Oaxaca as if they were treasures. I'd always admired crafts but the skill and artistry I encountered in Mexico inspired me to subsequently design housewares out of ceramics, tin, and glass. I am insistent that my reinterpretations maintain the integrity and richness of each regional tradition.

By this time, my individual taste and style had clearly emerged, so it felt appropriate to parlay my affinity for interiors and furnishings into a career. I enrolled in Sotheby's American Fine & Decorative Art master's program. I thought it would equip me with the academic credentials I needed to pursue a life in design, and I was right. The deep immersion course brought us into contact with a network of experts, curators, scholars, appraisers, dealers, and conservationists. We deconstructed furniture, analyzed woods, authenticated canvases under black light. Given entree into private collections, we crisscrossed the country examining paintings, sculpture, furniture, ceramics, glass, silver, and textiles. As I soaked up the multilayered itinerary I simultaneously fell in love with turn-of-the-century modernism. I also discovered a correlation: the more I studied, the greater my appetite to learn.

I spent the next couple of years running Aero Studios, the retail extension of Thomas O'Brien's studio in downtown New York. Thomas has a classic design vision that's part traditional and part midcentury modern. He reinvigorates everything he collects or repurposes, often transforming the generic into something exquisite and he's incredibly adept at articulating his thought process. My time at his firm was like a hands-on educational course.

For the following five years I applied the skills I acquired at Sotheby's by acting as director of the Lin-Weinberg Gallery. Andy Lin and Larry Weinberg, seasoned experts in international design, were part of a very small coterie of dealers who were instrumental in elevating the stature of vintage modernist furnishings. I had access to their extensive furniture, ceramics, textile, and art library, which was filled with current and out-of-print reference books and I took full advantage of it. Reading, researching, and

authenticating was an integral part of my job and I was in heaven. I derived huge amounts of pleasure from art directing the look of the store and breathing new life into museum-quality pieces when I curated the gallery's exhibition spaces at antique shows.

I started my own interior design firm in 2001 with the motto Curate, Don't Decorate and a mandate to create livable, meaningful homes that have intrinsic value. My work cohesively draws upon my experiences in the worlds of nature, art, and design and I consider it a privilege to be able to earn my living by enhancing people's everyday lives.

Over the years, I've kept my wits sharp by acting as an independent advisor to collectors of early-twentieth-century decorative arts, but in 2005, with writer and curator Bruce Willis Ferguson as my sounding board, I ventured into the world of contemporary design. I cofounded Design Miami with Ambra Medda after I realized fine arts galleries had the exclusive on showcasing furnishings from the postwar to contemporary period. After plowing through mounds of research I asked star designers and a host of international blue-chip galleries who specialize in furniture, decorative objects, and art to present work.

Their heavily vetted submissions became the inaugural set of exhibitions that ran in conjunction with Art Basel Miami Beach. Our Designer of the Year, Zaha Hadid, created a site-specific installation in one of Miami's historic buildings while we finalized the logistics on an extensive array of discussions, panels, and forums. By opening night, the now-annual fair felt like a feast, a hybrid of an intensive design workshop, and the most entertaining party I had ever attended.

I also cofounded Design Exchange, a support organization for novice interior designers who need advice on launching their careers. This year, I'm expanding the concept and the community by extending membership to contractors, developers, and architects.

As a codirector of the design council for New York's Museum of Arts and Design, I'm immersed in the work of established and up-and-coming designers and artisans and I see collaboration as a keystone of my work. When I trace my early affinity to nature and see it evolving into my current relationships with craftspeople, clients, design professionals, and artists, there's an obvious trajectory, as if my life has come full circle. The carpets, wall coverings, rugs, furniture, bathroom fixtures, and lighting I've designed as well as the boutique hotel I'm currently planning all feel like an extension of my childhood fort building. Without realizing it at the time, my life experiences conspired for me to become a designer.

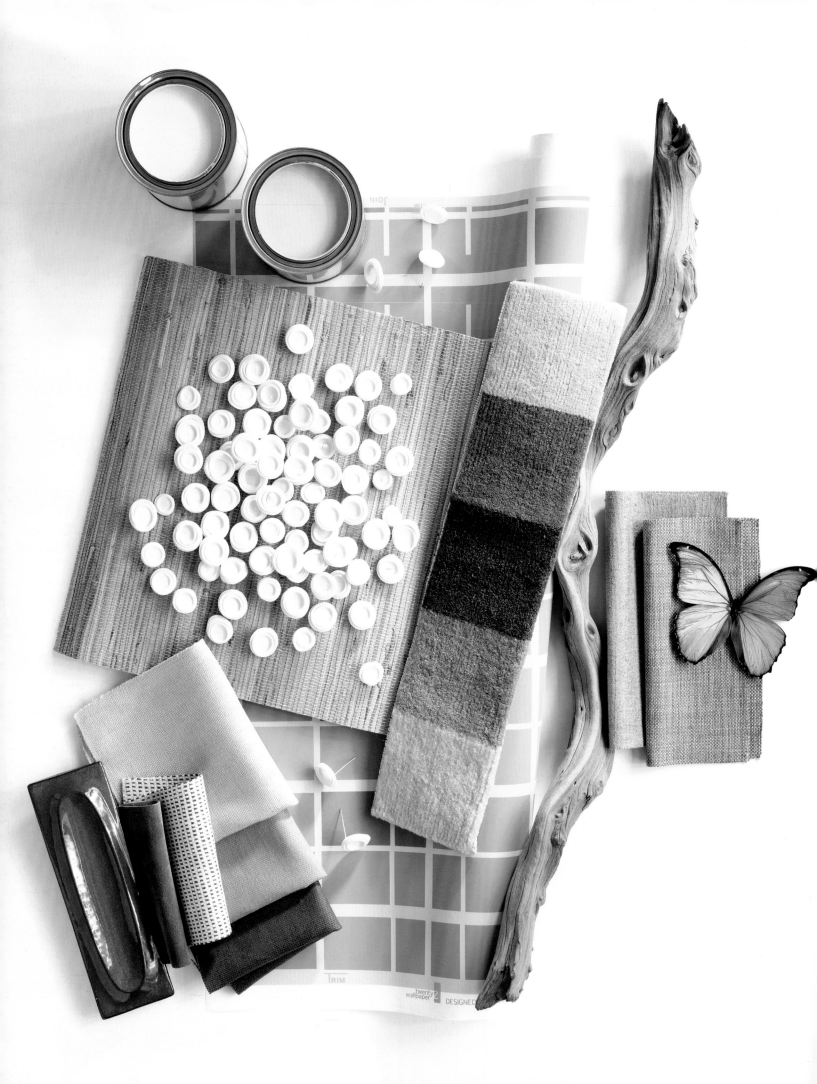

color AND pattern

Colors, like features,
follow the changes of the emotions.
Pablo Picasso

at the age of five, when my girlfriends were cooing over pink, I was jazzed about orange; a box of crayons seriously gave me goose bumps. So it's no surprise that I chose the very vibrant combination of kelly-green carpeting, a Marimekko bedspread, and carved Mexican furniture painted sunflower yellow for my childhood bedroom.

Color and pattern are eloquent agents for change because they instantly and dramatically alter our perceptions of a room's size, shape, and personality. With that in mind, select them with equal amounts of confidence and caution. If used badly, colors can clash and pattern can create discord in a room, producing the opposite of the intended effect.

Painter Josef Albers says, "In visual perception a color is never seen as it physically is." Color mirrors and reflects its surrounding surfaces—which is why you can never let a paint chip dictate an entire room's color scheme. Instead, mark off three 12-by-24-inch panels with painter's tape and test-coat three different shades of a color you like. Evaluate each panel's reaction to natural and artificial light throughout the day and evening. Maybe the shade darkens alongside the floor's ebony stain? Maybe it's too cool a contrast for the room's warm-toned woods? The same method works for wallpaper: pin up a large swatch and evaluate its compatibility alongside the material you've chosen for your curtains. Does its large repeat dwarf your favorite chair? Maybe it's destined to hang on one wall only and not all four?

Think holistically. See a room's walls, ceiling, and floor as a continuous surface and consider painting it in shades of one color. Monochromatic spaces are captivating, particularly when they have dimension—achieved by painting the color at full strength on the walls and at half or quarter strength (diluted with 50 or 25 percent white) on the trim, ceiling, and doors. Or, for a chic depth of field, try a monochromatic family of matte, shiny, and lacquer finishes.

If you have difficulty settling on a primary color, consult a color wheel. Cover two-thirds of a space with your color of choice, and then paint or wallpaper a single wall in its contrasting, complementary color. The result is like an unexpected—but very welcome—guest strolling into the room!

bridgehampton beach house

BRIDGEHAMPTON, NEW YORK

This house for developer Michael Hirtenstein is just minutes away from long stretches of beach, hydrangea-filled gardens, and vivid green polo lawns, yet when he first purchased it, it felt isolated from its picturesque surroundings.

Due to dark, structural wood rafters, the living room felt gloomy and vertical mullions on the windows shielded the sun and obscured the beautiful scenery. We replaced all the windows and painted the rafters and beams white, allowing daylight to pour in uninterrupted, to be reflected throughout; views of wildflowers became part of the interior itself.

Nature is referenced throughout the house in homage to its bucolic setting. In the dining room, a Murano glass chandelier and Vistosi sconces resemble iridescent shells; a ceramic wall treatment looks like Queen Anne's lace flowers; ceramic drums, used as bedside tables, might have been carved from white coral.

I reimagined each of the six bedrooms as suites in a boutique hotel and gave myself license to play. I designed active geometrics for all the carpets but kept to a monochromatic pattern or solid color for all the walls and custom bedding—this helps to ensure that nothing overpowers at eye level.

Textile designer Judy Ross helped to conceive the custom carpet—its aqua, citrus yellow, and green palette draws the outdoors in. The modern mix of furniture includes sun-parched drift- and petrified-wood coffee tables; a pair of Vladimir Kagan swivel armchairs; Hans Wegner's iconic Papa Bear chair; and a David Weeks chandelier.

Previous pages: A freestanding sculpture by Jerome Abel Seguin energizes a corner of the room. The artist created its seven-foot-high tendrils by submerging vines under the sea and twisting them together so they could take on the movement of the waves. A midcentury armoire and a Dunbar sofa establish the space's midcentury mood.

if your house
is located in a peaceful,
bucolic setting,
pay homage to the site
by referencing nature
throughout

Modular sculpture *Aggregation Ceramic Pieces* by Masami Tsuchikawa floats over a nature-inspired Stark wallcovering and above a vintage driftwood lamp.

my tastes have become
   more subdued over time,
   but georgia o'keeffe's
famous saying,
      "i found i could say things
with color and shapes
            that i couldn't say
any other way,"
      has always resonated
with me

The tones of artist David Winter's paper
Butterfly, right and above, are echoed in this
guest bedroom's vintage sunburst chair
and ottoman, Desiron twin beds, Tibetan
rug designed by Suzanne Sharp, and custom stools. The Boi Sconce by David Weeks
is a modern piece with midcentury appeal.

*I'm rooted in the Southwest.
I still think of its dusty olives,
siennas, and rusty browns
as "my colors."*

Custom-designed bedding sets off the graphic lines of twenty2's Acco wallpaper and contrasts pleasantly with the playful bubbles of Eboniste's bedside table. A vintage pendant lamp, rewired to modern codes, adds a final hit of texture to the space.

Giò Ponti's tile work in the Hotel Parco del Principe in Sorrento inspired the custom geometric rug in the master bedroom. Raised striations are reminiscent of a sandy beach; a five-armed Serge Mouille sconce loosely resembles the form of a starfish, and the walls are a very particular shade of Mediterranean blue.

central park west apartment

Michael Hirtenstein, a huge fan of mid-twentieth-century modern design commissioned me for his 3,000-square-foot rental apartment and gave me only two months to finish the job! Customizing furniture alone often requires several months! Commissioning cabinetry, individualizing draperies, or specifying a rug is an involved process and talented woodworkers, upholsterers, or artisans usually can't turn things around that quickly. Besides, I always want to find furnishings that fit clients like a tailored suit, and that simply takes time.

The good news is that Michael was able to clearly express his needs, likes, and dislikes. He's drawn to wood and glass, is ambivalent about conventional art, and entertains with a vengeance. Above all else, he wanted his spacious three-bedroom apartment to be fun and informal to compensate for a stressful job.

Because he often throws parties, we situated the dining and living areas opposite each other in the largest room, where guests can appreciate a pulsating, floor-to-ceiling view of midtown—as mesmerizing as a fireplace at night. A semicircular Vladimir Kagan sofa sits low on a splayed walnut base and offsets the room's symmetry and 10-foot-high ceilings.

In the dining area, a long bench opposite 1950s string-backed chairs is more refreshing than a conventional matching setup, and bronze butterfly joints give the tabletop some glint to complement the glass wall décor. There wasn't enough time to commission a studio rug, but as luck would have it, we fell in love with a sample from Zoë Luyendijk, an abstracted swirl of autumnal shades.

Michael's ability to be direct, his heightened sense of style, sharp eye, and appreciation of craftsmanship sped up the design process and we completed the job in record time.

The floor-to-ceiling window provides an exciting view of midtown and Central Park, and serves as the room's focal point.

Previous pages: A monumental glass sculpture formed from interlocking cast-glass tiles repurposed from a vintage room divider was chosen for the dining area to spar with the nearby view. Rather than stand it on the floor as it was intended to be displayed, we dismantled it and reconfigured it on the wall with brass armatures. Once mounted, the pieces fit together to make a gloriously rhythmic arrangement.

strive to create a livable, meaningful home of intrinsic artistic value

Cascading discs of glass in rainbow hues trickle down the clustered form of an eye-popping Vistosi chandelier, left.

Pieces from different periods and provenances coexist happily in this hall, right. A 1960s Swiss side cabinet supports West German vases of the same period; the ensemble is crowned by a scalloped-edge, glass-framed French mirror from the 1930s.

Previous page: A curvaceous wall-mounted cabinet, crafted from black walnut by Pennsylvania cabinetmaker Phillip Lloyd Powell, gives the main living space an eye-popping focal point.

Buckles on 1940s Hermès poufs originally owned by Jeanne Lanvin are referenced in custom pillows by Lauren Saunders, right. An armless sofa in a neutral cream sets off these decorative elements and the David Maisel print above.

Geometric ceramic tiles by Roger Capron inspire the master bedroom's subtle color scheme of mustards and grays, opposite. A Giancarlo Piretti club ottoman bench from the 1970s adds a playful coda to a bed that begins with a textured cowhide headboard.

greenwich village apartment

Calibrating the amount of natural light that seeps into a room is important because light is a vehicle for emotion. Or as Anton Chekhov so eloquently put it, "don't tell me the moon is shining; show me the glint of light on broken glass."

For some reason, modern architects who revere light and slot as many windows as possible into their projects shun curtains when they are, in fact, a noninvasive way to alter a room. Curtains draw attention to a room's periphery and ceiling height, alter its proportions, round off harsh angles, and add a touch of poetry.

When existing clients asked me to design this West Village penthouse, we decided the living room windows needed color and a sense of theatricality. They occupied the entire length of one wall so they had presence, but they lacked character and personality.

Privacy and excessive sun weren't issues here, so custom-designed, stationary wool panels—as opposed to drapes with pull cords— were a good solution. Static or not, a treatment should never weigh windows down: I steer clients away from fussy fabrics with pleated headers or any fabric that balloons or puddles on the floor.

To give the series of panels form and movement, textile designer Judy Ross and I came up with a slightly formal, undulating pattern stitched in rust-colored silk onto a creamy wool. Unlined so light can filter through, and sized so their hems just skim the floor, they create a double illusion of weightlessness. They are wide enough to draw closed, but they stack aside gracefully.

Sculpted, tailored curtains need only simple hardware, so we installed one continuous rod and attached each panel with rings.

conceal AND flaunt

*Design is not making beauty,
     beauty emerges from selection,
affinities, integration, love.*
     Louis I. Kahn

a harmonious living space is as beneficial to our health as good food and exercise. At the core of that harmony is strong, decisive editing. For good reason, one of the tenets of feng shui is the elimination of clutter. Unencumbered space is a universal luxury and clutter not only reads as chaotic, but it also physically and visually decreases a room's volume. There's no perceivable flow or rhythm in a jam-packed décor, whereas rooms that only contain the bare essentials are uninviting and alienating. Finding the right balance between the two is essential.

When I edit a room I stand back and take it in as an architectural whole before I zero in on the details. My advice is to consolidate rather than scatter belongings. View books, CDs, and DVDs as a cohesive library or a unified collection and confine them to one area, grouped by size, title, or author. Install shelves up to the ceiling. Consider spreading a horizontal shelf unit across an entire wall if a space lacks drama.

Be scrupulous about possessions—in general, the modernist credo "less is more" holds true—so if you don't love it, lose it! Make it a habit to turn seldom-used gadgets and rarely worn clothes into thrift-shop donations. Smart storage, credenzas with doors, bedside tables with drawers, and coffee tables with shelves are invaluable in rooms of any size.

On entering a room, our eyes continuously scan across and back unless there are focal points for them to land on. Pianos, fireplaces, and sofas obviously provide those points because of their imposing size. An artfully arranged collection—of shells, ceramics, masks, or anything you choose—also provides strong visual interest if it's refined periodically and showcases intriguing or rare specimens. It takes a firm hand and a practiced eye to decide what to keep and what to feature prominently.

Fine art elicits a response—that's why it's often central to my designs. At times a show-stopping chandelier, a chair with an interesting silhouette, or beautifully executed embroidery on a pillow can also become a powerful focal point. Any well-crafted item can give as much emotional satisfaction as a sculpture, painting, or mural.

essex house apartment

NEW YORK, NEW YORK

Artist Barbara S. Gross, my client, is a well-known jewelry designer with an Auntie Mame personality and an impressive body of work, sculptures, and canvases that are characteristically vibrant and modern.

For her midtown Manhattan apartment, the furnishings needed to highlight the art, so we singled out Barbara's most beloved pieces and designed rooms around them. Two of her works played pivotal roles. The first, an abstract sculpture carved from black steatite, prompted us to cover the living room and vestibule walls with ebony plaster. Once we had top-coated them in wax, they took on a reflective sheen, as if the spaces were lined with silky, satin ribbon. Truly glamorous, the dark, dramatic walls are the perfect foil for the metals and other reflective media Gross uses in her work. The ceilings in both spaces have low soffits so we tinted them a soft gray and applied a muted silver stain to the floors.

The second important piece, a vibrant canvas of intermingling circles and triangles, titled *Broken Hearts*, received pride of place in the living room. Edward Fields extracted its DNA and designed a textured rug of the same motif—pile heights change according to color. The painting's imagery emerges again, this time referenced on pillows upholstered in velvet Emilio Pucci skirt fabric and on a pink chaise strategically positioned in front of a large window so that Gross can glimpse couples strolling through Central Park below. We created a unique design for each room, rather than adopting a unified style for the apartment.

In Auntie Mame's words, "Life is a banquet!"

Broad, curving planes on the artist's own sculpture, right, are echoed subtly in the custom-designed rug below.

Bold swaths of color in a painting created by the client and pillows created from the owner's collection of vintage Emilio Pucci skirts, opposite, welcome visitors in the foyer and hint at the equally commanding spaces beyond.

Previous pages: We selected storage that had equal amounts of allure and function. A large lacquered coffee table has recessed niches; the sides of cubic cocktail tables lift up like garage doors to uncover inner shelving; a mirrored Paul Evans desk cantilevers up to reveal a secret compartment.

The rule of thumb here was that every practical piece should hold its own against the bold artwork.

bright fabrics, accessories, and furnishings animate otherwise dark interiors

The many facets of the owner's wall and table sculptures catch light as it permeates into the dining room's interior. A Marie-Claude de Fouquières dining table from Todd Merrill Antiques is surrounded by Paul Evans Skyscraper dining chairs from the 1960s and a Quarter Circle sofa by Vladimir Kagan. A Gaetano Sciolari chrome pendant lamp adds a crowning metallic touch.

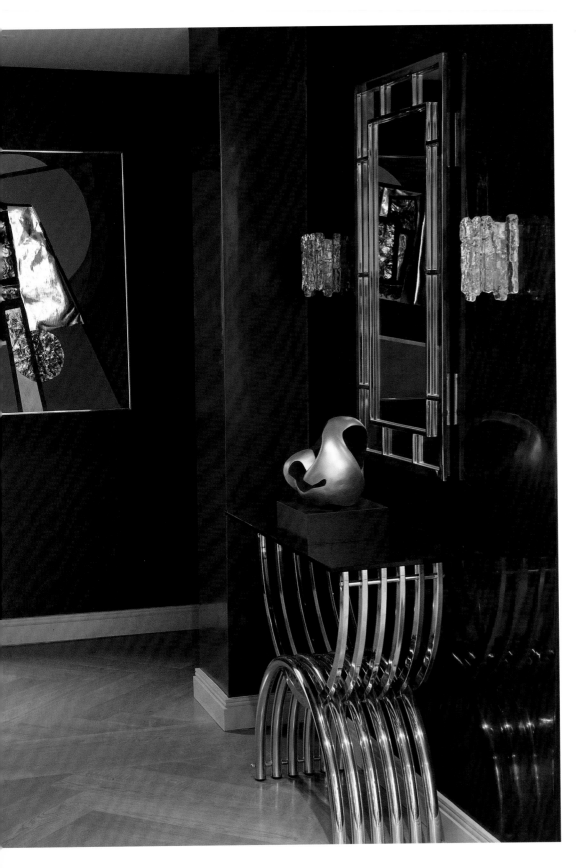

An American mirror with an openwork brass frame found at John Salibello Antiques, left, proves the perfect match for an Eccola console fitted with a new black glass top.

Rectangular patterns begun by the studded facade of a highly lacquered American sideboard from the 1970s are continued in a pair of Italian table lamps from the same era, opposite. Reflective surfaces on the Milo Baughman black patent leather swivel chair and a Karl Springer side table add compelling glints of light and shadow to the room.

The materials used in this bedroom shimmer from incoming natural light.

Luxurious silk velvet walls in the master bedroom set the standard for other sumptuous materials including a curvaceous Murano glass lamp, below, a custom bed designed with Michael Tavano, and Grosfeld House off-white lacquer cabinets dating to the 1940s.

A 1934 Samuel Marx mantel surround in painted wood and glass and gilded with silver leaf is the bedroom's centerpiece, opposite. The rug, designed by Zoë Luyendijk, is based on the owner's impressionistic canvas *Green Landscape* and uses nine materials, including banana fibers.

for any designer,
the ultimate reward
   is hearing a client say,
"i feel like i've lived here
             forever"

Exuberant cherry blossoms printed on Clarence House wallpaper begin a theme of heavy lacquer and chinoiserie for this guest bedroom sustained in the vintage headboard, mirror frame, and the 1940s Mont-style nightstands. Christopher Spitzmiller ceramic lamps and an Edward Wormley narrow bench upholstered in velvet bookend the scene.

chicago townhouse

CHICAGO, ILLINOIS

These clients, a financier and a choreographer/dancer, asked Jon Heinert of Wheeler Kearns Architects to turn a quarter of their 3,000-square-foot Chicago townhouse into a library, screening room, gym, and a ballroom to enable them to host benefits, fund-raisers, recitals, and performances.

To delineate the ballroom clearly from other spaces, Heinert lowered a section of the ceiling and joined it to two freestanding walls that are at right angles to a 50-foot-long wall of windows. He paneled this "room within a room" with fiddleback sycamore, which cleverly hides a mass of utilities and provides a streamlined, organic envelope for furnishings.

Rooms come alive when people inhabit them. Any large room designed to hold dozens of people will be in danger of resembling a hotel lobby when the party's over if the proportions of its architecture and furniture are not also conceived with more intimate gatherings in mind.

In any large space, the shapes of individual pieces are as important as their functions—people move around and can therefore take them in from many vantage points. A mix of strong curves and handsome lines also offsets a room's angular architecture and humanizes its scale by providing midrange interest.

The biggest challenge, finding a focal point for one of the sycamore walls, was solved when a monumental sculpture by postwar abstractionist Claire Falkenstein appeared at auction. It spans eight feet and, once mounted, its cluster of wires and chunks of glass conjure up shooting stars. Lauren Saunders used that same celestial imagery in the hand-crocheted swirls and beams of light she hand embroidered onto the pillows for the adjacent sofa.

*Intimate groupings
of furniture always help
to break up a large space.*

Small, animated arrangements of chairs
and sofas are easily reconfigurable setups
perfect for hosting different types of events.

A three-light lamp dating to the 1970s by Italian house Crystal Arte presents a dramatic entrance to the ballroom, left, dominated by Claire Falkenstein's wall-mounted sculpture. Frattini lounge chairs, a floating-back Dunbar sofa and custom pillows by Lauren Saunders await some of the owners' frequent guests.

A classic Giò Ponti console table and pair of sconces welcome guests to the foyer, right, while a FontanaArte chandelier lights the way to a cozy Marco Zanuso settee bedecked with custom pillows by Judy Ross and fronted by a Karl Springer coffee table.

The carpet's mottled pattern resembles stars—an homage to Vincent van Gogh's *Starry Night*. Midnight-blue draperies subtly hand-embroidered with the Chicago sky-line and four Milo Baughman swivel chairs whose circular brass backs glow at sunset complete the color scheme.

art provides
     the hierarchy of color
and pattern in a room:
     a motif or graphic element
from a painting
          can be blown out of scale
to inspire pillows,
               a rug design,
     even a mural

Wood and leather accents, below and
right, warm up the library. Lounge chairs
by Borsani flank a mid-twentieth-century
Italian rosewood circular table to create
one seating area; a sectional sofa by Gilbert
Rohde creates another.

Subtly sinuous arms on the full set of Edward Wormley for Dunbar dining chairs set off the staunchly geometric presence of a Paolo Buffa for Eccola sideboard from the 1950s.

Straightforward circle and square motifs are enhanced by the introduction of color and subtly abstract throw pillows in this guest bedroom, below.

Dot patterns both overhead and underfoot, opposite, lead the eye beguilingly down a long hall, enlivening what is normally a merely functional space.

Wide horizontal stripes in tan, brown, and blue, above, create a restful backdrop for pattern introduced in the bedding, carpet, and the Fantoni lamps on the side tables.

Masculine geometric forms and colors permeate a guest bedroom, left. Bedding by Wallter and a Desiron bed play on the blue-gray tones found in the wallpaper and rug.

function AND flair

Have nothing in your house that you do not know to be useful or believe to be beautiful.
William Morris

function makes everyday life smooth, or, as modernist architect Le Corbusier put it, "A house is a machine for living." My interpretation of that phrase is that successful interior design supports our activities and enhances our lives by anticipating our behavior.

From the moment we wake up, we each have our own unique pattern. We get out of bed on a particular side; we choose one stool over another as we drink our morning coffee or tea; we throw our keys in a certain spot. Spend time reflecting on your routines and let the choice and placement of your belongings accommodate and preempt your needs.

Analyze how you plan to use a space and devise a floor plan that weighs the room's architectural assets alongside its shortcomings. Know that rooms are like body types: there is no perfect shape or size. A simple shift in expectations can sometimes help to downplay a room's flaws.

Certain tried-and-true design rules apply in confined, high-service areas like bathrooms. A pair of sconces flanking a console mirror gives off the most balanced light for shaving or applying makeup. Cabinets that float rather than those that reach the floor maximize space. Towel rails and wall hooks should be strategically placed and close at hand.

In a living room, the layout is more open to interpretation. Aim for artful with strong doses of common sense. Clusters of two or three mismatched armchairs are more intimate and visually arresting than a boxy combination of two identical sofas and a rectangular coffee table. Portable side tables large enough to hold a couple of drinks or a book or two give a room visual fluidity. Throw pillows "comfy up" a sofa and double as visual magnets that pull in a room's color scheme.

Cater to your idiosyncrasies and commit to your lifestyle choices. I upholstered my entire apartment so that my beloved dog, a Spinone affectionately known as Goofy, could have free reign. I devised an off-white color scheme to match his fur and used practically bulletproof fabrics that don't show wear and tear when he curls up on the carpet or falls asleep on the sofa with muddy paws. Define comfort in your own terms.

downtown apartment

Artwork plays an aesthetic and practical role in my work, especially when it's used as a focal point. An abstract canvas can either stimulate or calm the senses while it corrals together and echoes a room's colors, shapes, or textures.

The clients who asked me to work on this 2,500-square-foot apartment in downtown Manhattan owned a bold, biomorphic painting by Rex Ray. When I discovered Elson & Company had also translated one of his graphics into a hand-knotted Tibetan rug, it was an obvious purchase to make, and one that inspired the color scheme and furniture contours in the living room. I extracted a portion of the rug's pattern and asked textile artist Judy Ross to embroider it onto pillows. This series of connections to Ray's work gave the living room visual depth as well as a psychological layer of familiarity and comfort.

Certain isolated shapes are both uplifting and purposeful. I often design loose curves or concentric circles into a carpet so that once installed, the shapes delineate or separate parts of a room like an invisible wall. Alternately, a structural swoop in a sofa's back or seat can be used to demarcate a seating area.

The apartment's tour de force lighting—a free-form composition of fifteen of David Weeks's enameled Boi lamps—claims an entire wall of the living room. The sconce heads swivel so that when switched on at night they can be redirected in infinite ways, as if they were participants in an interactive art installation.

a diminutive painting,
a delicate vase,
even a favorite
armchair's fabric
can serve as
the inspiration
for an entire color scheme

The kitchen's small footprint is an ode to the ingenuity of ships' galleys.

Top-of-the-counter cabinets, right, are outfitted with glass and lit from within. At night they flood the kitchen's back wall and the overall effect of hardware-free Corian cabinets is monumental and sculptural.

Indirect light, opposite and right, is the perfect distraction for guests who might otherwise glue their eyes to their hosts' cutting boards or stovetop.

connect to the spirit
of the objects you live with,
and only keep those
that resonate with you—
the choice is bound
to be right
if it's from the heart

Textiles designed by Judy Ross, below, complement the vivacious glass patterns in the headboard and the pendant lamp custom blown by Michael Anchin.

Abstract upholstery on a T.H. Robsjohn-Gibbings chair dating to the 1950s, right, complements the fluidity of a James Lecce painting. A Paul McCobb birch dresser completes the period mood.

central park west apartment

Generally, when couples discuss color, one of them is invariably more vocal than the other. In this case, the husband and wife had equally strong convictions, so we had many lively talks about paints and fabrics.

This was my second project with architect Glenn Leitch. The rapport we established earlier working together on Elie Tahari's store in the Hamptons continued here and we collaborated on everything from space planning to materials.

The apartment is L-shaped, with a monolithic column dominating the hall opposite the entry, so there was no natural flow from one room to another. The wavy outline of Alvar Aalto's iconic Savoy vase provided inspiration for the solution. With Leitch, I devised an undulating wall, which wraps itself around the offending column to gracefully divert incoming guests away from the kitchen and into the living room and dining room beyond. We commissioned sculptor and furniture designer Jim Zivic to clad the structure's facade with strips of chocolate-brown leather.

I had my clients' color choices for the living room—peach, golden raisin yellow, pale blue, and light green—in mind when I consulted artists and rug designers Janis Provisor and Brad Davis. Their artisanal gallery, Fort Street Studio, has a gorgeous inventory of meticulous hand-knotted carpets, all inspired by the abstract watercolors they paint. The luscious pile of their rugs treads like suede and their wild silk construction has a unique luminosity that helps to divert the eye away from the living room's low ceiling. Once we settled on which watercolor to use as inspiration we customized its colors and manipulated its concentric circle to make it radiate outward so that its translation into a rug would pull together the seating area.

Lauren Saunders's pillows, right, provide the room's most prominent patterns, created of loomed mohair over velvet. The transparent overlays of striated color have the integrity of artwork.

The walls are kept neutral, opposite, while the sofa and chairs, upholstered in solids, add color and complement the rug.

color contributes to a project's flow as much as architecture or furnishings —it energizes or pacifies

Subtle details for the eye abound in this dining room, right. Eight vintage Bega and Gottardi chairs upholstered in a muted slate blue pick up the silver-colored, wishbone-shaped table support in the apartment's dining room while a vintage Roak chandelier and a colorful abstract painting by J. Lubin draw the gaze upward.

Previous page: A roomful of important mid-century pieces look at home in modern Manhattan. A Vladimir Kagan cloud sofa, armchairs by Poltrona Roxa, a John Widdicomb freeform coffee table, and a vintage pendant lamp by Donzella create an assembly that Goofy, a Spinone Italiano, declares quite cozy.

To conceal an awkwardly placed structural column in the entryway, left, I conceived of wrapping it in undulating strips of leather. Jim Zivic and I created one of the apartment's most notable features out of what was previously a blemish.

Highly polished metallic tiles with a strongly rectilinear pattern, opposite, are softened by the addition of a spiraling Scandinavian chandelier and a biomorphic cowhide rug designed by Kyle Bunting.

Dark reflective materials and a leather wall inspired by the shape of an Alvar Aalto vase add a sense of luxury to the entryway.

The kitchen's wooden materials installed by Bulthaup are reprised in the vintage dining chairs and the round table's custom tulip-shaped base. A vintage Mazzega chandelier provides an ethereal counterpoint above.

Any beautifully crafted object can give as much emotional satisfaction as a sculpture, painting, or mural.

color and pattern instantly alter our perceptions of a room's size, shape, and personality

Soothing muted earthtones lend an air of relaxation to this bedroom. Custom-designed bed linens and accent pillows by Lauren Saunders coordinate with a carefully curated selection of glass vases and the simple, clean lines of Roman shades. A pair of vintage FontanaArte sconces emit soft, relaxing light for reading.

Glass tile, below, selected to complement the lively stripes on the wall of this guest bedroom, at right, accentuate the tones of fuchsia and blue picked up in the Marc Pascal pendant and custom-designed headboard.

*A room's colors should work
with adjacent rooms, hallways,
or neighboring spaces.*

Geometric shapes in warm, inviting colors
are introduced to this guest suite via trape-
zoidal tiles by Angela Adams for Ann Sacks,
a fun wall treatment crafted from various
Benjamin Moore paints, and custom pillows
by Judy Ross.

curate AND decorate

*Every object tells a story
if you know how to read it.*
Henry Ford

when we infuse meaning and emotion into everyday objects they enhance our lives and draw us into a dialogue. We begin to treat the chair that supports us when we read or the desk drawer we open several times a day as if they are more than mere objects: we treat them as vehicles of self-expression.

Objects that tell a story are often the most interesting—and certainly the most valuable—so when I furnish a home I approach the assignment as both a curator and a decorator. Functionality is a must, but before I preoccupy myself with intrinsic value, craftsmanship, artistry, and form, I pose the most important question: Will this piece speak to my client? Will it satisfy her tastes? Will it reflect his interests? Objects that resonate invariably have a talismanic energy that's palpable.

Curating a respectable collection of objects requires a connoisseur's mindset. Furnishings with good provenance are sound investments that hold value. Part of the curatorial process is exposing clients to galleries, auction houses, and other avenues of distribution. Whenever I want to assess the substance of a prospective buy I reference the handbook antique dealer Albert Sack wrote decades ago. His authentication process, which still holds true today, evaluates a piece's age by its symmetry, rhythmic flow, and woodgrain and is practically foolproof.

I'm passionate about preservation and maintenance. Like any good custodian, I love breathing life back into the things I find. For example, if a wicker chair seat is overly worn, I'll track down the original caner; if a chaise or ottoman needs reupholstering, I use fabric that's close to the original. The quick-fix solution—altering an original design by say, staining or lacquering a table to fit with a particular scheme—is never the best choice. Assembling your cohesive collection at home means focusing on pulling together individual pieces that have a particular spirit so they come together as a family.

It is vitally important to be scrupulous when vetting contemporary design; all objects should be sourced from reputable galleries and dealers. Limited editions from current designers are, after all, the antiques of the future.

kent lake house

After I've worked with the same clients more than once, a bond akin to family kicks in, which is the case with Charles and Xiomara Scheidt. So when they bought this wooded property an hour north of New York City and we began collaborating for a second time, it felt like I already knew their tastes by heart.

The site borders a calm, secluded lake, but the original 1940s bungalow that came with it was dilapidated and sad-looking, so they commissioned Joseph Tanney and Robert Luntz of Resolution: 4 Architecture to level the structure and build an efficient, compact 2,400-square-foot house on the original foundation.

Charles and Xiomara had differing visions for their getaway retreat. He wanted a rustic Adirondack cabin while she wanted a hip-looking loft. The architects' material selection appeased them both—local stone and cedar siding for him; lots of glass, translucent fiberglass, and rolled steel walls for her—and comes across as at once traditional and modernist.

On a crisp fall day, the autumnal foliage is visible through ten-foot-high, floor-to-ceiling glass walls and appears to be nature-made wallpaper. These very red, yellow, and orange leaves outside inspired the house's entire earthy color scheme—which creates a stunning contrast to the interior's wood finishes.

The Scheidts wanted timeless furniture, so our search led to classic pieces that create a soft-angled, curvy, mid-twentieth-century collection. It offsets the rectilinear mullions and masculine steel panels in the great room. Resolution: 4's striking wall materials, patinated steel, and grainy woods were focal points in themselves and virtually made artwork seem redundant. Nevertheless, the steel wall above the fireplace clearly needed a visual anchor and the inexpensive abstract painting was an inspired auction find.

The house's glass windows, right, create a wallpaper of foliage that transforms with the seasons.

A 1960s enameled chandelier, opposite, whose fixtures rustle in the cross breezes to mimic the movement of falling leaves, decorates the dining room.

Previous pages: An amoeba-shaped coffee table by T. H. Robsjohn-Gibbings felt destined to partner a tufted sectional sofa by Edward Wormley. A shapely pair of Harvey Probber chairs swivels to take in all the views. By shopping wisely and staying within budget, we splurged on a handful of artisanal touches, including embroidered pillows and a hand-forged fire screen.

When walking this site, we picked up red, orange, and yellow leaves, and the house's earthy color scheme was born.

Furnishings created by Paul McCobb in the 1950s provide this guest room with an air of restrained elegance and simplicity. His chest of drawers and headboards are set off by a geometric rya rug, a pair of vintage ottomans, and a Muriel Coleman table lamp.

soft-angled curvy
furniture offsets
rectilinear elements
to give a room
extra dimension

*Nature is a friend and teacher
who continues to inform my
interior design work every day.*

A collection of favorite *objets*, below, crafted in naturalistic forms and of natural materials prepares the eye to take in the beautiful lake and woodland site, visible through the floor-to-ceiling window.

Midtoned wood present in the form of a 1960s Danish desk and Hans Wegner chair, opposite, accentuate the beauty of the actual woods just outside. An articulated desk lamp by Gilbert Watrous and a telescope add the only industrial touches.

miami
townhouse

MIAMI, FLORIDA

These clients are both collectors. She had warehouses of her mother's vintage furniture, mainly Italian—with some pieces dating to the 1920s—by Giò Ponti, Ico Parisi, Osvaldo Borsani, and Ettore Sottsass. He had a vast collection of contemporary photography, paintings, and sculpture by local Miami artists as well as international art stars. I was assigned the enviable task of furnishing their Miami guest house around so many amazing pieces.

Displaying any collection, small or large, whether it's ephemera, memorabilia, furniture, accessories, or art, calls for ruthless editing and restraint—a particularly daunting task with so many potential choices. In this case, function dictated my decisions to a large degree but color, alongside proportion, materials, shape, and texture also played a vital role in each grouping.

Off-white walls are traditionally used in galleries and museums but often leave a home feeling unfinished. However, here, in the boxy architecture of a recently built house, the white walls, ceilings, and floors serve a double purpose. They act as a cool-headed antidote to Miami's hot and sultry weather and supply a neutral backdrop that presents the art and furniture as if it were one cohesive collection, floating in a field of white.

Hanging art is subjective and site-specific, so the first step is to throw away any formula. Instead, be intuitive and work from the assumption that wall art is best viewed at eye level. With a large collection of art or photographs, it is helpful to play around with placement by cutting out and hanging cardboard or paper templates of every frame or canvas on the wall in the arrangement you want to pursue. For various sizes of frames, one option is to tape the largest template in the center of the space and work outward—I use that technique so often that I'm known for walking around job sites wearing rolls of tape as bracelets.

124

*White walls, ceilings,
and floors cause the art
and furniture to "float."*

Inspired by James Turrell, the artist whose
built rooms play with our perceptions of
space, I extended the white onto the ceilings
and floors, opposite, so that the physical
presence of light was discernible and envel-
oping. The furniture's aged olivewood, oak,
ash, lacquer, and brass become even more
distinctive in the space now, and every pattern, color, or piece of art pops.

vintage midcentury
modern furniture
shares a natural affinity
with contemporary art

A collection of glass in vibrant, rainbow colors finds a home on a Silvio Cavatorta shelving unit and a Giò Ponti sideboard, opposite and below. An eye-catching chaise in red by Osvolado Borsani and an intricate tabletop sculpture by Curtis Jere complete the room's curated suite of objects.

Displaying any collection, small or large, calls for editing and restraint.

A colorful display of Holmegaard vases, right, is curated so that the unique form and color of each is highlighted by its placement in the group.

Paired cabinets by Giò Ponti, opposite, draw extra attention for their reversed color schemes but identical design; a freeform wall sculpture by Curtis Jere hangs above, its many discs offsetting the cabinets' strongly rectilinear lines.

The organic, asymmetric shape of a Carlo Mollino–style wall lamp accents the stylized curves of a Kofod-Larsen chair, above. A simple 1953 Giò Ponti vanity complements the other two pieces in scale and period.

Mette Tommerup's *Digidentity* begins the dining room's theme of bold midcentury forms, opposite. A Tom Dixon table is accompanied by red Ico and Luisa Parisi dining chairs, and a unique Italian credenza from the 1950s anchors the far wall.

whether it's embroidered,
painted, printed on velvet,
or woven in silk,
a room's pattern creates
a musical crescendo
for the space

In the children's room, below and opposite, cheerful bands of playful hues provide the color, while the furnishings composed of basic geometric shapes are kept to a simple white the kids won't outgrow. A Ferruccio Laviana Fly suspension lamp for Kartell adds an outsized pop to the ceiling.

A pair of Charlotte Perriand stools inventively fill the space normally allotted to a chaise in this bedroom, and relate in color and number to the wooden Giò Ponti wall-mounted headboards. The rug is by Niba Collections, and the custom bed cover was designed by Judy Ross.

art AND interpretation

Art is a collaboration between God and the artist, and the less the artist does the better.
André Gide

in my experience, truly creative people are generous with their ideas and relish the opportunity to work alongside like-minded colleagues whose work they respect. It's gratifying to watch a project evolve and improve when there's a meeting of minds with client, designer, architect, contractor, and artisans working toward a common goal. The trick is to ensure that each person feels they have creative freedom within the specific boundaries or confines of the overall project.

The best designs happen when the architect and interior designer confer at a project's inception because then there are no stops and starts, the process stays fluid, and one decision affects the next. A joint outlook on materials and finishes, from bath tiles to exterior cladding, establishes a visual rapport that serves as a firm foundation for every aspect of the design process that follows. Then, nothing is fractured. Minute details are considered with the big picture in mind.

When it's a challenge for clients to articulate their aesthetics I ask them to define their personal taste by taking cell phone snapshots of things that strike a chord, or by scouring magazines and the Internet for images they find appealing. Over the years I've kept track of things that inspire me, and I now have shelves of binders bulging with scraps of paper, reminding me of particularly pleasing art, landscapes, fashion, and architecture. I leaf through them every now and then—whenever I need a visual cocktail.

Clients' scrapbooks are a starting point for a dialogue, but are certainly not for interpreting literally. I examine the shapes, patterns, colors, periods, and textures they give me—from surface appeal to symbolic meanings—and create a style that's unique and familiar to them because it is a distillation of things they love.

In addition to collecting visual stimuli, I follow the work of new and established artists, artisans, and craftspeople; I keep track of talents uncovered at art fairs, auction houses, museums, flea markets, and in art magazines. When I'm in search of an original take on a mural or want a particularly innovative rug design, I can consult my lists to choose an artisan whose skill sets will enrich the project with an extra layer of meaning.

showtime
dexter room

It's easy to draw parallels between dining rooms and stage sets. Dinners, like plays, are choreographed performances with a balanced cast of characters and a beginning, middle, and end, broken down into two or three courses or acts. At a dinner party, the evening's hero isn't the protagonist, however: it's the chef.

Metropolitan Home magazine and Showtime television commandeered an empty nineteenth-century Gramercy Park townhouse and asked a select list of interior designers to create show rooms for lead characters from any of the latter's top-tier TV series. I chose the dining room and Dexter Morgan of the show *Dexter* as my fictional client and commissioned and directed twenty-one artisans and artists to create a functional room that could double as the set for a play entitled *Dinner at Dexter's.*

In Showtime's series, Dexter is a blood-splatter analyst. He is a conventional husband and father by day but moonlights as a vigilante serial killer, who stalks the guilty, administering justice with compulsive, fatal precision.

I studied Dexter's habits and idiosyncrasies as I would any of my actual clients', but, in this case, I watched episode after episode and dissected his behavior. The show's set decoration and lighting are incredibly meticulous and symbolic, so I wanted the room to reflect that same attention to detail.

Every designer, ceramicist, cabinetmaker, painter, sculptor, and videographer who worked on the room fine-tuned their work to fit into my overall concept; the room evolved into a tongue-in-cheek replica of Dexter's psyche. In the end, the room became a multimedia performance piece, antiseptically white with splashes of red. So many creative voices came together and gave birth to something truly unique.

In this show room, right, vintage red vases and a Beast console table and mirror by Stephen Antonson are offset by eerie art. K. B. Jones created the blood spatters with oil-based enamel paint and red threadwork in a nod to Dexter's day job; the piece above the fireplace was created by Nava Lubelski and consists of thread, paint, and ink on canvas cut to reveal the wall behind.

A dancing web of fifteen hundred dismembered doll parts hand cast with EasyFlo liquid plastic, opposite, greets visitors entering the space while a chandelier formed from wine glasses, cables, and wax rope draws the them deeper into the room. Each dining chair is individually hand-embroidered by Leah Picker with a custom slash on the front and spatters on the back.

attention to detail was paramount to simulate the show's precision and symbolism

Clockwise from top left: Blood-spattered dinner plates by KleinReid are the perfect counterpart to chargers by Nadeige Choplet; flatware with various essential pieces missing are another nod to Dexter's gruesome hobby. Guests are sure to remember which dining chair is theirs, thanks to unique embroidered slash and spatter marks on each. Candlesticks by Stephen Antonson are meant to evoke human vertebrae. Glassware by Thomas Fuchs contains red detailing best described as a vein.

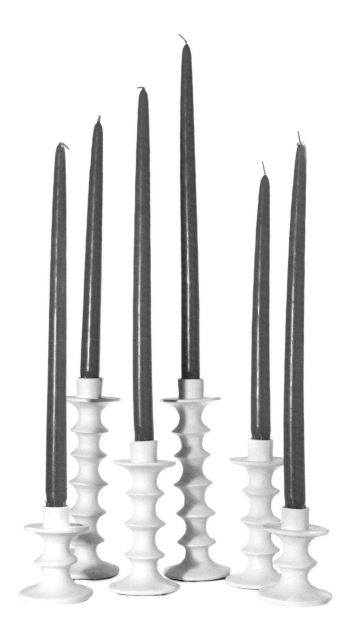

kips bay decorator show house

In the design world, Maya Romanoff is legendary. A fine artist and born innovator, for the past forty years he has married technology with ancient craft-making to design a vast array of wall coverings including laser-cut veneers and treatments made from exotic paulownia trees, kenaf plants, hemp, felt, mother-of-pearl, and capiz shells. The Cooper-Hewitt National Design Museum recently accepted one of his designs, a flexible glass bead surface, into its permanent collection.

When I decided to participate in the 2009 Kips Bay Decorator Show House transformation of a townhouse designed in 1922 by C.P.H. Gilbert, I had in mind a raised, three-dimensional application of Maya's printed and painted wallpapers. I sketched out my assigned area, the staircase wall that linked the second and third floors, and, inspired by the playfulness in Jean-Honoré Fragonard's painting *The Swing,* created a motif of trailing branches. Then I remembered a magnificent vase of magnolias I'd seen in one of the galleries at the Frick Collection and I fleshed out my drawing with plump blossoms.

I asked talented paper artist Jo Lynn Alcorn to help execute the installation. The finished mural exceeded our own expectations. On a logistical level, it served as a sorbet course for anyone transitioning between the myriad of design styles on the second and third floors. On an emotional level, it was a piece of poetry, causing many to literally stop in their tracks. One journalist described Jo Lynn's work as alchemy. At first glance, people speculated that she'd sculpted the flowers from wax, resin, or even porcelain. They couldn't believe she had cut them out of wallpaper.

The magnolia leaves were constructed from seven different paper patterns and required ladders, scaffolding, and a crew of nine to install. Maya Romanoff's studio custom colored and cut the branches and hand painted all the leaves while Jo Lynn Alcorn meticulously cut the magnolia petals by hand, down to every last spiny stamen.

craft AND soul

*The hand is the window
on to the mind.*

Immanuel Kant

i have a reverence for nature and I'm drawn to objects crafted from organic materials—particularly when they show signs of the earth or the artisan's hand.

A talented artist has the ability to use a natural raw material and release its energy. Tooling, technical expertise, and cultural tradition come into play here and contribute layers of meaning. My grandmother, an artist, was particularly versed in naturalism and mineralogy and my father, a fine art collector with a passion for material culture, collects Anasazi and Mimbres pottery. Throughout my childhood I was surrounded by groupings of stones and ceramics and absorbed all the stories these ancient objects told.

That same sense of spirit can also be present in a newly blown knob of blue glass with a translucence that appears to contain the depth of the ocean. It's hard not to have respect for a material's longevity. Take bronze candlesticks, woven baskets, or loomed textiles: well cared for, they'll outlive us all.

When introducing crafts into a room, consider their commonality. Resist the temptation to automatically group them according to geographic or cultural origin. Instead, focus on characteristics of material, form, color, and proportion and keep refining the palette until everything extraneous is gone. To me, grouping collections is a methodical process that's both visceral and mindful.

The eye always views an object in the context of its surroundings and, as any gallerist knows, the energy and space around a work of art or craft or a piece of furniture is as important as the energy within. Any object that disrupts the overall harmony of a grouping should be removed so that the surviving pieces have room to breathe. Be vigilant about the hierarchy of shapes and make sure no single piece upstages another. Once that balance is achieved, a sense of beauty and simplicity will follow naturally.

As a final gesture, connect to the spirit of the things you live with and experiment by only keeping things that have resonance. The choice is bound to be right if it's from the heart.

kips bay decorator show house

The first time I participated in the Kips Bay Decorator Show House, in 2007, the esteemed interior design fundraiser that benefits a local New York Boys and Girls Club, I customized practically every piece of furniture, accessory, and surface. After all, I was my own client and only had myself to answer to!

My process began, as it usually does, by listening to an empty space. I'd just come back from Big Sur reinvigorated and relaxed, so I decided the room should function as a lounge. I called it *Rites of Spring*, in a nod to Stravinsky's iconic ballet and the season.

The rectangular space was 500 square feet, and a 14-by-12-foot glass wall separated it from a top-floor terrace. Unfortunately, a low, solid wall enclosing a staircase sat in the room's core and everyone who walked upstairs had to turn to make their entrance. At first, that struck me as awkward and untheatrical, but as I began working in the space, I gradually changed my mind. I actually liked the element of discovery. If you dislike something structural that can't be changed, my tip is to simply make friends with it.

Sea, sand, and sky, as well as numerous abstract allusions to spring influenced the room's decorative finishes. A painting from Josef Albers's *Formulation* series, a study of muted citron, cobalt, and diffused gray-blue inspired the palette, and the artist's theories about color and perception—"abstraction is real, probably more real than nature"—were silent contributors to the space. Apart from a few vases of budding flowers and foliage, the scheme of abstraction prevailed.

After the show house opened to the public, it was rewarding to see that people were noticeably drawn to the space. I guess the concept worked!

The serpentine curves of a long Milo Baughman sofa direct the room's energy and flow as if it were a signpost.

Previous pages: The undulating striations of paint and plaster on the walls bring to mind the horizons of lava-glazed German pottery's freeform coloration.

Brightly lacquered discs of blue, green, and yellow form the custom frame for a circular mirror, below, that radiates cheer. Its colors are picked up again in the custom window treatments by Maki Yamamoto, opposite.

A 1950s-era wall-mounted cabinet by Phil Powell and Paul Evans does double duty as a bar and display space. Lemon stools are given an exuberant twist with abstract embroidery by Judy Ross.

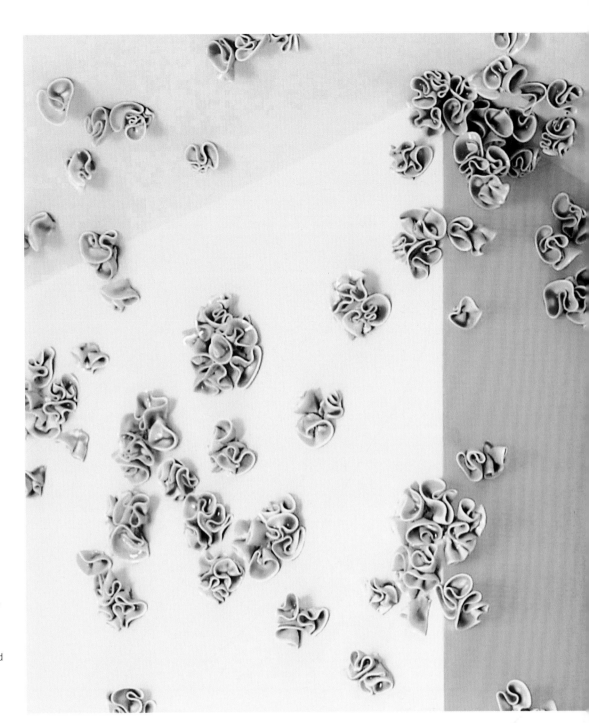

Porcelain pinched into delicate petals by Jennifer Prichard, right, forms an abstract sculpture that unexpectely lilts around corners and flutters up to the ceiling.

Artisanal glass medallions from southern Mexico provide more impact when gathered into a custom chandelier, opposite, than they ever could alone; its circular motif is repeated subtly in the seats of the chairs and base of the table.

An object's worth and significance come not from its monetary value but from the intent and skill that went into its creation.

conceptualize a room's floors, walls, and ceilings as one continuous plane to establish a feeling of rhythm and flow

west chelsea loft

Architect Ate Atema and I teamed up to reconfigure this former gallery in the heart of New York City's arts district. An earlier conversion had carved out two bedrooms, a kitchen, and an office, but the remaining area in the 4,000-square-foot space was open and felt too raw to be considered a true home.

Ideally the layout of a large room should feel comfortable and intimate for one person yet simultaneously welcome a crowd. And that's a challenge—it's like asking a person to be introverted and extroverted at once!

It takes time to figure out what makes someone tick aesthetically so visits to design fairs and art galleries help provoke a dialogue. Books on interiors, articles on design, and photos of furnishings dotted with Post-it notes also fuel an exchange of information.

The client wears customized suits, ties, and shirts, and I interpreted that as a clear sign that he respects process, materials, and detailing. He showed interest in a 1960s bench built by master woodworker Shizuhiko Watanabe that was coming up at auction and also mentioned Andy Goldsworthy, the artist and poet who uses nature as his medium. Those two influences led to an interior with clean, organic lines, honest craftsmanship, and unadorned materials.

A simple request—for a place to take morning tea—illustrates the client's love of order and his delight in everyday rituals, and actually became a pivotal part of the overall furniture scheme. We sited the low, square tea table in the center of the loft and its presence reverberated outward, defining all its neighboring areas.

Natural hemp and wool rugs complemented the characteristics of the raw silk in the shoji-screen panels. I balanced the screens' dark frames with textural, neutral walls and floors. All the room's humble materials achieved a unified sense of glamour.

*I always try to find furnishings that
fit a client as well as a tailored suit.*

The owner travels internationally a great
deal and appreciates craftsmanship from
a wide span of cultures, left, so we decided
to reflect that interest in the new décor.

The client's passion for reading meant that
a library, opposite, required pride of place.

collecting art and décor
from a wide span of
cultures reflects a love
of international travel and
artisanal craftmanship
that guests grasp instantly

Shoji screens are fitted with silk-and-pandanus-cloth fabric. The walls are covered made with raw pigments mixed into a clay-and-milk base.

The floors were created by hand troweling cement, plaster, and pigment to the original gray cement floors, producing a surface that absorbs and deflects light like suede.

a love of order often naturally leads to design with straight lines and a simple palette

Nubbly gray wool sobers a Hans Wegner Papa Bear chair, left, enough to tie into the rest of the apartment's palette while adding a moment of playfulness to the room.

Antique Indian doors lead the way to the master bedroom, opposite, where a French industrial mold for an airvent radiates calm. Its circular form is reminiscent of Asian motifs without being literal, but a nineteenth-century lacquer cabinet and Esri Afghan rug add touches of authenticity that relate to the owner's heritage.

Architect Ate Atema created modern mill-work in the form of a contemporary desk, opposite, that fulfills the client's need for simplicity while providing him with plenty of much-needed workspace.

A tree-shaped candelabrum sculpture welcomes guests in the foyer.

*I'm drawn to objects crafted
from organic materials—
particularly when they show signs
of the earth or the artisan's hand.*

muses AND mentors

the immortal exhortation to "sail away from the safe harbor. Catch the trade winds in your sails. Explore. Dream. Discover," uttered by Mark Twain, might have served as a mantra for all the people who've inspired my life and work. Whether they chose architecture, interior design, painting or ceramics, each one of them took the road less traveled and envisioned the ordinary as extraordinary. Each one was instinctively committed to their personal aesthetic and they pursued it fearlessly. They all defy categorization, which is a prerequisite to uniqueness, and their work is timeless and life-enhancing because it came from a deep-rooted passion. It was a means to self-exploration. I can only aspire!

From stretches of water to museums, the near and faraway places that invigorate me and replenish my spirit all have a pronounced sense of light or color. They have the power to draw me into the moment and move me emotionally, which is why I consider them to be transformational. They also keep me in awe of nature and reinforce my belief that the world is essentially a joyful place.

oia, mark rothko, and kohler tiles

One of my favorite places in the world is Oia, a small fishing village on the Greek island of Santorini, where houses are carved directly out of porous volcanic rock and the blue domes of churches dot the landscape. When the Aegean Sea is particularly calm at sunset, a truly transcendent golden light washes over the whitewashed hillside. Witnessing this almost surreal phenomenon first-hand gave me a new appreciation for the color and light fields in the paintings Mark Rothko began producing in the late 1940s. Their colors merge and almost vibrate in their luminescence. Critics at the time saw them as revelations and Rothko felt they embodied his spiritual side. I thought about all the shades of Oia blues and Rothko's merging colors when I designed my line of tiles for Kohler.

maya romanoff and tie-dyed wallpaper

Tie-dye is an ancient, labor-intensive method of resist dying that's common to many cultures in Africa, Indonesia, and India. The earliest example of a tie-dyed fabric dates back to Peru around 500 A.D., and there is also evidence that the Japanese used the technique to decorate kimonos as long ago as the eighth century. Its layers and intensities of color reminded me of abstract dreams and rediscovering them in Maya Romanoff's archives brought back happy memories of tie-dye from my youth. In traditional tie-dye, a textile is stitched or tied into a pleated or twisted formation before it's submerged into a vat of color. Maya hand-dyes and folds his papers to mimic the authentic process. He asked me to contemporize a handful of his patterns as a way to commemorate his fortieth anniversary, and I came up with four versions, including a half-plaid and a kaleidoscopic snowflake. These were exhibited at Bergdorf Goodman during the celebration.

nature, elie tahari, and tappio wirkkala

I can't be blasé about nature. It's God's art and I'll never stop falling in love with plants, butterfly wings, clouds, and flowers. They are wondrous. When I first met fashion designer Elie Tahari, I was pleased to discover that we spoke the same language; he used driftwood, shells, and natural fibers to articulate his vision for the East Hampton boutique I designed. Architects Piero Lissoni, Nicoletta Canesi, and Glenn Leitch blew out the walls of a former post office, installed smoked wood floors, and coated the walls with Venetian plaster so the building seemed to emanate light from within. Needless to say, the collection of mid-twentieth-century furniture we chose looked amazing against that backdrop. Nature also appears in a mystical way in all of Tapio Wirkkala's designs. He broke down the boundaries between art and craft and experimented with every material imaginable. His glasswork abstracts Finland's wintry landscapes; my favorite Wirkkala pieces resemble dripping icicles.

mary jane colter

A true pioneer, Mary Jane Colter trained to be a designer and architect at the turn of the twentieth century, when men dominated both professions. Fred Harvey employed her for twenty-one years and she created a series of hotels throughout the Southwest, many of which now have historic landmark status. At La Posada, Hopi House, and the Phantom Ranch buildings at the bottom of the Grand Canyon, she managed to synthesize a number of indigenous styles with modern tastes without diminishing their authenticity. She was deeply interested in history and maintained strong connections with the American Indian culture while she created commercial projects that were playful and dramatic. She will forever be one of the grandest ladies of the Southwest.

giò ponti

It's hard not to be inspired by Giò Ponti—he excelled at any discipline where he tried his hand! One of Italy's most important architects and industrial designers, his bottles, sinks, sofas, silverware, tiles, and lamps became staples of twentieth-century households. He was also a poet, philosopher, and editor and he founded *Domus* magazine as an expressive forum for his thoughts and ideas. He painted frescos in some of his buildings and even designed costumes for La Scala. His Superleggera chair, as weightless and shapely as it is sturdy, has become a true icon of the era. His work is graphic and playful, sexy and chic, whimsical and pared down, all while showing a sophisticated sensitivity to color and line. His passion for design and the joy he felt in the act of creation are evident in every piece he produced.

vladimir kagan

Vladimir Kagan is a living treasure. He is an artist with an unparalleled understanding of form, and his medium happens to be furniture. The biomorphic, fluid shapes he created decades ago still look ahead of their time! He moved from Germany to the United States in 1938, studied architecture, opened a store in New York in 1948, and designed furniture for locations as varied as the United Nations Headquarters and Disneyland. Several of his pieces are housed in permanent museum collections around the world. His work is timeless and arguably endures because he approaches it from so many sides—as architect, designer, and retailer. He never prioritizes form over comfort and he incorporates nature's graceful shapes into every object. I feature his furniture as prominently as artwork in my interiors, especially when it's upholstered in fabrics embellished with crewel work designed by his very talented wife, Erica Wilson.

louis comfort tiffany

Like many of the people who inspire me, Louis Comfort Tiffany began with a fascination with nature that he first sought to express as a painter, and found his true calling later in the field of decorative arts. Known mainly for his unique glasswork, he experimented continuously, inventing both glassmaking techniques and finishes. He created jewelry, mosaics, pottery, and leaded glass windows and lamps. His world travels influenced his designs and taught him to think unconventionally. He was also an interior designer, famously reinstating glamour to several rooms in the White House. He took over his father's jewelry and silver business in 1902 and turned it into Tiffany & Co. as we know it today—an American bastion of design that successfully celebrates artistry on a commercial level.

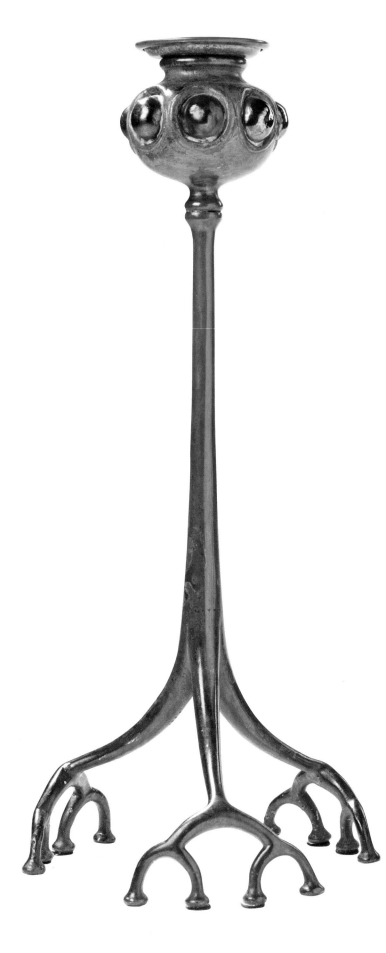

german
ceramics

Popular during the 1930s Arts and Crafts movement was a type of German ceramic that I absolutely love. It has intense earthtone colors, cratered textures, and a mix of matte and gloss glazes that drip and melt into each other like volcanic lava. The thick glazes often produce unusual imperfections such as bubbles that pop and pit to reveal underlying colors. The character of each vase stems from these "flaws."

rya rugs

Ryas—vivid, monochromatic rugs—first originated in Sweden in the 1600s, when they functioned as bed covers. Since then, they have evolved to serve mainly a decorative purpose and often depict stripes, flowers, or animals. Their popularity and form has also spread to other cultures, where similarly constructed rugs function as prayer rugs and burial blankets. Made by artisans from long-pile wool, they are hand-knotted and stitched together on their backside. Their rustic designs, variegated colors, and shaggy expressiveness make them perpetually endearing.

josef albers

Abstract painter Josef Albers was also a teacher who wrote extensively on color and redefined art education in the twentieth century. He designed furniture, decorative surfaces, and facades, worked as a typographer and photographer, and came to the United States when the Nazis forced the closure of the Bauhaus in 1933. He disagreed that "pure color" exists, and illustrated how our perception of it changes dramatically as it absorbs or reflects its environment. His disciplined approach to composition influenced generations of artists and formed the fundamental philosophy of the op art movement. His writings taught me that color is alive and, thanks to him, I never choose a color in isolation, but always consider it in the context of its surroundings.

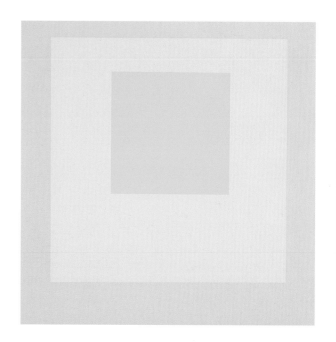

james turrell

James Turrell's work is at once simple and profound, perceptual and celestial, modern and ancient, and he is a master at expressing insight and poetry. He elevates light to a spiritual medium. His enclosed rooms where the ceilings are totally open to the heavens and his ingenious methods of projecting light to give it the discernible weight of sculpture make us appreciate this everyday substance in an entirely fresh way. In 1979 Turrell bought the Roden Crater, a two-mile-wide extinct volcano in Arizona, and is slowly transforming it into a heritage or pilgrimate site. This vast site contains various paths and gates that lead directly to the lip of the crater as well as a surreal bronze staircase leading up to an open sky, and is an ever-evolving work in progress.

beatrice wood

Born in California, Beatrice Wood studied painting in France, spent years acting on the stage, founded a dadaist magazine with Marcel Duchamp, befriended Man Ray and Francis Picabia, and was immortalized as the female character in François Truffaut's film *Jules et Jim*. She came to pottery in her forties when she couldn't find a teapot to match two of her favorite plates. Over the course of a sixty-year career, she developed distinct luster glazes and patterning for her ceramics and sculptures. She was a devoted follower of the Indian philosopher Jiddu Krishnamurti and when asked to account for her passion and vitality she said, "I owe it all to chocolate and young men." She wrote extensively and recorded her adventurous life in eighty-five years' worth of diaries.

bardo museum, tunis

While studying with archeologist and art historian Howard David Soren, I fell in love with the Bardo Museum in Tunis, Tunisia. The structure is built on the site of a thirteenth-century palace and it houses a magnificent collection of Roman mosaics. Floors, frescos, and ceilings originally built for sumptuous villas depict mythological characters, hunts, and harvests, and some date to the second and third centuries. I'm like a kid in a candy store here because you can actually touch and walk over these ancient relics. They even inspired me to take mosaic glass courses when I returned home.

antoni gaudí

I am perpetually moved and inspired by Antoni Gaudí's conviction, perseverance, and absolute artistry. Due to a prolonged childhood illness he spent a lot of time alone, walking out of doors, and everything he later designed including furniture, hardware, and stained glass, showed his reverence for and fascination with nature. He designed many buildings in Barcelona, but his life's work and obsession was clearly the city's cathedral, Sagrada Família, begun in 1883 and left unfinished at the time of his death in 1926. Construction has continued in fits and starts as political events and funding has disrupted the process, but it is slated to be completed in 2026 to commemorate the one hundredth anniversary of his death. Gaudí developed innovative engineering to stabilize the church's structure of sensually carved walls. A hybrid of Gothic, art nouveau, and traditional Catalan architecture, its uniqueness was mocked during Gaudí's lifetime but it is now acknowledged as a masterpiece.

frida kahlo, emily carr, and georgia o'keeffe

Frida Kahlo was a revolutionary who found the inner strength to overcome physical disabilities, dedicate herself to her art, and pursue an unconventional love life. The vibrancy, emotion, and subtext of her paintings is as stirring today as it was decades ago. She refused to suppress her femininity or her life force; she saw herself as "a ribbon wrapped around a bomb." The same era produced two more equally strong women artists, Emily Carr and Georgia O'Keeffe. Carr's compassion for the indigenous people of the Canadian Pacific Northwest and her deep spiritual connection to nature inspired her postimpressionist portraits and landscapes. O'Keeffe found her true voice when she moved to New Mexico and began painting the high desert plants and flowers she encountered on her daily walks.

acknowledgments

I grew up surrounded by my talented grandmother's paintings, my father's collection of fledgling artists' works, and my mother's flare for detail when decorating our home and organizing parties. Throughout my childhood I developed an eye for my surroundings and learned to appreciate both the beauty in objects as well as the history and meaning behind them. My past has truly molded my future as an artist, a curator, and a designer. So thank you to my ever-supportive family.

I want to extend my gratitude to my clients for letting me channel their visions, for their trust in my insight, and most important, for their enthusiasm: our collaborations make each project unique and special.

Thank you to the architects and contractors I have had the pleasure of working with; their visions, hard work, attention to detail, and team spirit have made every project an exciting and memorable experience. No project would have been the same without each and every one.

My great appreciation goes to my amazing staff that is forever on duty. Their commitment to excellence, hard work, and daily enthusiasm has helped create countless amazing results.

I have had the great pleasure to collaborate with many fine artisans, whose one-of-a-kind creations have helped to establish unique interiors over and over again. I would like to extend a huge thank you to Gregoire Abrial, Jo Lynn Alcorn, Stephen Antonson, Angelica Bergamini, David Brooks, Kyle Bunting, Steve Butcher, Jon Cory, Jane D'Arensbourg, Patrick Gallagher, Tori Higa, Kevin Inkawhich, KB Jones, Chris Klapper, Nava Lubelski, Osmundo, Jennifer Prichard, Toby Revis, Maya Romanoff, Judy Ross, Lauren Saunders, Marcus Tremonto, and Susan Weinthaler, Dustin Yellin, and Jim Zivic, to name just a few.

I would also like to say a special thank you to the many people who are very dear to my heart and have supported me so beautifully in the industry: Fred Bernstein, Michael Bruno, Deborah Burns, Michele Caniato, Jim Carroll, Anna Cosentino, Kipton Cronkite, Jim Druckman, Nancy Epstein, Bruce Ferguson, Bobby Gain, Al Harary, Holly Hotchner, Craig Kellogg, Eve Krzyzanowski, Andy Lin, Eileen McComb, David McFadden, Sarah Natkins, Julia Noran, Daniel Quintero, Amy Rosi, Jason Sheftell, Jennifer Skoda, Michael Tavano, and Marilyn White.

A very special thank you to my dear friend and public relations guru, Katharina Plath, whose love and support have helped guide me through both business and life with soulful gentleness.

Thank you to Richard Wright who supplied me with many beautiful images for the Muses and Mentors chapter. And thank you to all of the talented photographers whose images are able to capture my vision.

And lastly, a very special thank you to all the people that made this book possible. In particular, Stacee Lawrence for her positive spirit, and enthusiasm, and of course, her patience. To the extremely talented Linda O'Keeffe, whom I respect dearly, for writing an interesting story and lending her keen eye. To Alba Contreras-Cedeno for her steadfast commitment in keeping the project going and to Katrin Lau for always knowing how to capture what to say so beautifully.

Thankfully, art is never-ending . . .

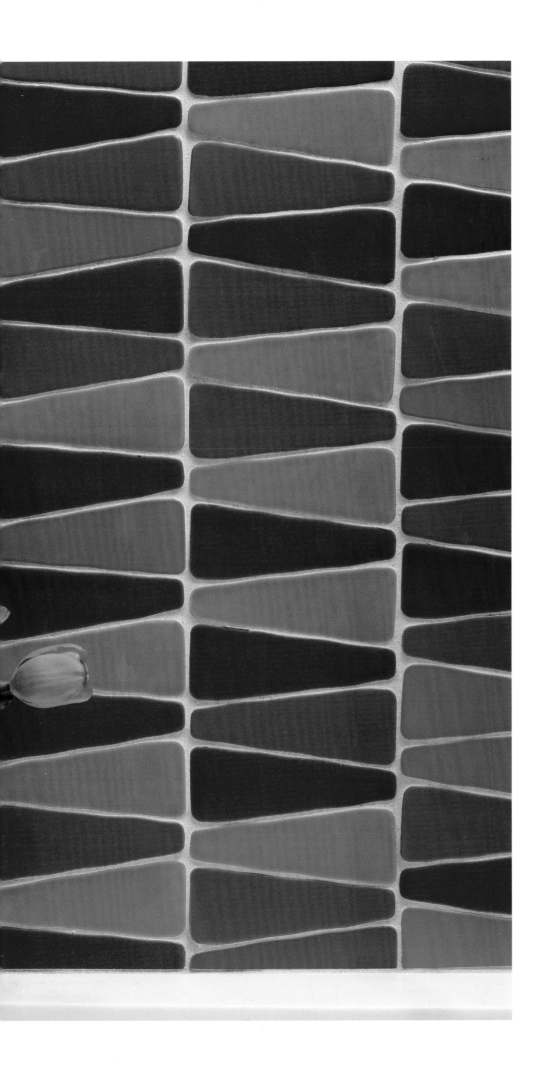

credits

Numbers refer to page numbers.

Melanie Acevedo 8, 11, 12, 124–25, 126, 127, 129, 130, 131, 132, 133, 134, 135, 136, 138, 139, 140–41, 182

Antonis Achilleos 14, 44, 80, 112, 142, 156

© 2011 Banco de México Diego Rivera Frida Kahlo Museums Trust, Mexico, D.F. / Artists Rights Society (ARS), New York; Photo Credit: Schawlkwijk / Art Resource, NY 212

Photo by Tony Cunha, Courtesy Beatrice Wood Center for the Arts/ Happy Valley Foundation 206 top, 207 right

Roger Davies 42–43, 83, 84, 86, 87, 89, 90, 91

© Fotosearch 208

© 2011 Georgia O'Keeffe Museum / Artists Rights Society (ARS), New York 213

Grand Canyon National Park #11422 191

Grand Canyon National Park #16950 190

Courtesy Hachette/Joshua McHugh 114–15, 116, 117, 118, 119, 121, 122, 123

Courtesy F.J. Hakimian 201

Giò Ponti Archives 193 top

Photographs Copyright © 2003 IMS Communications Ltd.; www.picture-gallery.com 209

© istockphoto / Dreef 211

© istockphoto / mbbirdy 185

Courtesy Vladimir Kagan 194 top

Courtesy Kohler 184

Hulya Kolabas 169, 176, 178, 179, 180

Joshua McHugh 115, 116, 117, 118, 119, 121, 122, 123, 170, 171, 172, 173, 174, 181

Bärbel Miebach 49, 50, 54

Permanent Collection: Beatrice Wood Center for the Arts 207

Kim Sargent 46–47, 48, 52–53, 55, 56, 57, 59, 60–61, 62–63, 64, 65, 66, 67, 68–69, 70, 72, 73, 74–75, 76, 77, 78, 79, 92–93, 94, 95, 97, 98–99, 100, 101, 102, 105, 106–7, 108, 109, 110, 111

Courtesy Maya Romanoff 187

Courtesy Royal BC Museum, BC Archives 213

Courtesy Elie Tahari 189

Kris Tamburello 4–5, 16–17, 18–19, 20, 22–23, 24, 26, 27, 28, 29, 30–31, 144–45, 146, 147, 149, 150 all, 151 all, 152–53, 154, 155, 158–59, 160–61, 162, 163, 164, 165, 167

© 2011 James Turrell; Photo credit: Florian Holzherr/Courtesy Gagosian Gallery 205

Vase, 1892–97 (glass) by Louis Comfort Tiffany (1848-1933) Cincinnati Art Museum, Ohio, USA/Gift of Alfred Traber Goshorn/The Bridgeman Art Library 197

Courtesy Wright 188, 192, 193 bottom, 194 bottom, 195, 196, 199, 202, 203, 206